Investing

The Power Of High-Level Investing Explained For
Beginners: A Guide To Financial Freedom Through
Investing

*(A Complete Guide To The Various Methods And
Applications Used In Trading)*

Ahmad Wieland

TABLE OF CONTENT

Calculating Returns On Dividend Stock Investments

Investing in stocks that pay dividends is a straightforward process. The more you comprehend of it, the less complicated it will appear. When constructing your portfolio and estimating your returns, you will frequently need to perform a number of computations. Before you go ahead and make this investment, there are a few things that you absolutely need to be aware of first.

The annual dividend yield is a percentage that shows the amount of dividends that are paid out for each share of stock that is owned as an investment. The corporations use this formula to evaluate how much of a return on investment you may expect to receive from purchasing dividend stocks. For example, if you buy stock shares with a value of $50 and receive

$2 in dividends, the yearly dividend yield will be 4% in this scenario. If you plan to subsist solely off of passive income, then you should invest in equities that generate the highest percentages of dividends.

The term "dividend growth rate" describes the rate at which your dividends continue to grow over the course of time. This computation is necessary in order to get an accurate picture of how quickly your income will increase in the years to come. Calculations of dividend growth rates are almost generally done on a yearly basis. To accomplish this, first calculate the dividend per share for the current year by dividing the total amount of the payout for the previous year by the amount for the current year.

The payout ratio is a measurement that determines the link between the total amount of dividend stock and the total amount of stock earnings. A high payment frequently indicates that the corporation is retaining a very small portion of its profits for the purpose of growing the enterprise. This should serve as a warning sign because the corporation may, at some point in the future, be required to cut the payouts in order to satisfy the requirements of the business.

When you are trying to make a living off dividends from stocks, the quantity of money you will receive on a consistent basis should be your first focus. You need to make sure that you buy a stock whose dividends are not going to decrease in the foreseeable future if you want to make sure that your passive income keeps growing over time. You must always keep this quality of good stocks in mind, as it is one of the features that makes up good stocks.

Dates of Dividends

When it comes to the dividend distribution, in addition to the calculations, there are a number of dates that are significant. For example, the date on which a firm announces to its shareholders that it will distribute dividends totaling a specific amount of money is referred to as the declaration date for the company. There is also the concept of the ex-dividend date, which denotes the final day on which an investor must hold stock in a certain firm in order for that investor to be eligible to receive a dividend payment from that company. The date on which the dividends are paid out to shareholders is known as the payment date for the dividend. The record date is the last date on the list, and it occurs far less frequently than the other dates. This date indicates the day on which a shareholder should be included on the record of individuals who are eligible to receive dividends. The record date is always the second business day after the date that shares are considered ex-dividend.

Comparing Growth Stocks To Value Stocks

When investors are searching for long-term strategies to apply in the stock market, one of the questions that frequently comes up is whether they should invest in growth stocks or value stocks. To begin, let's get a grasp on what each of these phrases actually means. A stock is considered to be growth if it increases in value over time due to capital appreciation. Therefore, if you invest in this stock, you are making a bet that the price of the stock will rise as the years and months pass. When purchasing growth stocks, investors have the expectation that their investments will increase in value over time, and that they will eventually be able to sell those holdings at a profit. Amazon is a wonderful example of a growth stock; its share prices have virtually skyrocketed, and it is currently selling at approximately $1,900 per share. This indicates that Amazon is expected to continue its rapid expansion. If you had invested in Amazon ten or twenty years ago, you would probably be grinning at the notion of it right now.

In the vast majority of cases, dividends are not going to be distributed by growth stocks. This relates back to the conversation we had in the previous : growth stocks are typically connected with companies that are themselves quickly expanding. These businesses are aiming to capture a significantly larger portion of the market and expand into additional international markets. As was mentioned before, this kind of businesses is more likely to spend the majority of their profits, if not all of them, into the expansion of their operations. This may take the form of constructing new production facilities, doing research and development, expanding their workforce, or opening up additional retail locations.

As a direct consequence of this, the vast majority of fast-growing companies do not pay dividends. Apple is one of the best instances of a company that follows this practice. Apple, on the other hand, is a rapidly expanding business. If you look at Apple's dividend payment, though, you'll notice that their yield is actually quite low. If I were looking for a stock that paid dividends, Apple is not the company that I would choose. Despite the fact that the company has a lot going for it, an income stock wouldn't be a good bet due to the fact that their yield is so low.

Undervalued stocks, often known as value stocks, are shares issued by reputable businesses that are now trading at prices that are lower than what the market suggests they should be. Consider the track record of the company in question in order to ascertain whether or not the stock in question represents good value. The performance of the firm, as measured by earnings, profits, and other metrics, is typically correlated with the price of the company's shares. If a firm has consistent profitability, year-over-year increase in revenue, and it pays a healthy dividend, then the stock of that company ought to be one that is enticing to investors. There are instances when the market pays little attention to a great number of companies for a variety of reasons. That translates to the fact that you can get them at a reduced cost. However, it requires some effort to locate and recognize equities that offer value.

To be categorized as a value stock, it is not necessary for a stock to have a history of consistently paying dividends. The primary characteristic of a value stock is that the stock itself trades at a price that is lower than its true worth. That is, the share price is much below what it should be given the state of the company's fundamentals. Warren Buffett, who is renowned as one of the world's most successful investors, is known for investing in value stocks.

When searching for value stocks, the price-to-earnings ratio is the most important factor to consider. Therefore, although this is likely to be a company that brings in a respectable amount of revenue and profits, its share price is going to be rather modest. A low price-to-book ratio is another indicator of a value stock's attractiveness.

It is not going to be possible for you to identify whether or not a stock is a value stock simply by taking a quick look at the price to earnings ratio of the firm. This is because the two metrics are not directly related to one another. You will not be able to do so by simply glancing at the price of the stock either. What you need to do is contrast the stock's price to earnings ratio with that of other companies in a comparable industry. To begin, you will need to be familiar with the standard price-to-earnings ratio for the entire stock market. However, it is far more crucial to be familiar with the price-to-earnings ratio for the industry in which the firm operates and to compare it to the price-to-earnings ratios of other companies operating in the same field.

Therefore, it is not possible to assess whether a stock is a value stock by comparing it to another company, such as Apple or Duke Energy, which is a utility company. To avoid making a pun, let's just say that your comparison is apples to oranges. Furthermore, you should avoid drawing comparisons between Facebook and United Health Care.

Nevertheless, you might contrast Apple and Microsoft, as well as Facebook and Twitter. Consequently, to continue with the pun, compare apples to apples. Compare the firm you're interested in to others in the same industry, for instance if you're looking at different pharmaceutical companies.

When it comes to stocks that distribute dividends, one of the signs that you may be looking at a value company is that they are going to be paying a high yield. This is because value stocks tend to be less volatile than growth stocks. The dividend payment split by the stock price gives you the yield as a percentage. Therefore, the stock price of an undervalued firm is going to be very low, but the dividend payment may be stable, which will result in a large yield on the investment.

However, a high yield is not sufficient evidence that the stock is trading at a discount on its own. You will need to compare a high yield to the price to earnings ratio, and then analyze how that company stacks up against other comparable businesses operating in the same market or sector. In addition to this, you should examine the yield in comparison to that of other businesses operating in the same industry.

For those interested in investing, value stocks present an opportunity. The primary reason for this is that you are going to have the opportunity to purchase equities at prices that are currently at or near all-time lows. Value stocks can be considered a bit of a gamble for investors who are traders with a short-term time horizon or who are seeking to profit from an increase in share price. This is due to the possibility that the stock price will not increase, in which case the investor will not be able to make a profit from the shares they own. However, if you are an investor in dividends, you do not need to be concerned about these difficulties. You will find that value stocks are of interest to you due to the fact that you will be able to purchase a value stock at a low price and still benefit from the high yields that are paid on the dividends.

That indicates that in order to achieve a specific level of income, you will be required to purchase a lower number of shares of stock than you normally would have done.

Others view value stocks as an opportunity because, at some point in the future, the market will acknowledge the fact that the firm is operating well if it continues to do so. That indicates that the price of the share will go up at some point in the future.

Value stocks are usually appealing to dividend investors since value equities are typically held by established businesses that pay dividends on a consistent basis.

To briefly summarize, a value stock is going to be characterized by having the following qualities:

The fundamentals of the company, such as earnings and profits, will be stable.

It is expected to have a low price to book ratio in addition to a low price to earnings ratio. You should evaluate the company's price to earnings ratio in comparison to that of other comparable businesses operating in the same industry and sector. Determine the average price to earnings ratio for the S&P 500 or any other index that the firm is included in. If the company is not included in any index, skip this step. Then you should contrast that with the firm. If the firm in question has a P/E ratio that is significantly lower than the index's average, this is a strong indicator that the stock in question is a value stock. Keep in mind that there are situations when an entire industry might be priced too low. In light of this, it is beneficial to check against the index in addition to looking at companies that are comparable.

When measured against other stocks in its sector, the dividend yield of a value stock is going to be significantly higher if the underlying company pays out dividends.

The day-to-day struggle to acquire more cash is something that the vast majority, if not all of us, are accustomed to. A hard business to operate, a career that consumes the best hours of the day, a mortgage, and children who believe that money can be made from anything are all factors that hinder us from pausing for a moment to understand how we might generate extra money outside of the usual nine to five workday.

I would like to disprove the common belief that putting in more effort would result in a greater financial reward. This leads you to fall into the common fallacy of believing that the only resource you have that can make you money is your time. This is the case in many situations. There is another option available to us. If you can break this pattern as soon as possible, you will have more time to make changes that will have an effect on the remainder of your life.

The tactic of the sloth that is discussed in this book

is one that must be carried out over a protracted period of time and calls for consistent dedication as well as self-discipline. There is no shortage of "financial growth gurus," but in all honesty, this isn't exactly rocket science. You can construct your first financial portfolio like a sloth, and ideally it will be the last one you ever need to construct.

Don't get the wrong impression. I have nothing against folks that are dedicated to their career and genuinely like what they do. Professions are very significant. When you first meet someone in a social setting, what question do you immediately want to ask them? "What kind of work do you do?"

Maintain both your employment and your career. There is no problem with doing that at all. However, rather than relying solely on your own efforts to generate cash, why not take advantage of the successes achieved by others? To start an investment portfolio with a significant amount of shares is the same as saying that. When you make an investment in Facebook by purchasing shares of the firm, you automatically become a shareholder in the business. You are able to make money off of the job that is being done by their thousands of employees. Every morning, thousands of alarm clocks in the Facebook offices go off to wake up engineers, customer service representatives, security guards, and even maintenance crews. This is done for one purpose: to boost profits for the corporation in which you own shares.

Making your own money is a satisfying experience for obvious reasons. However, at some point in your adult life, time will turn into a valuable resource for you. Building up your assets gives you the opportunity to begin earning from the time of others as well, which reduces the demand for you to rent out your limited time in exchange for money. The encouraging news is that accomplishing this won't be difficult at all for you. Today, starting an investment portfolio may be as simple as clicking a mouse button thanks to the advancements made in technology. It's really close to being magic.

Anyone who does not figure out how to make money while they are asleep will be forced to toil away their entire lives. (Depicted here is my wife nodding off while reading a book that I had written.)

In spite of the magic, it is possible that the value of your initial investment in exchange-traded funds (ETFs) would decrease over the course of the first few years. Does that imply that you have to take your money out of the market and wait for a good time to put it back in, or that you should allow yourself to become stressed out because your new portfolio continues to show losses? Absolutely not! It should come as no surprise that the stock market experiences both gains and losses. However, the past several centuries of economic history have also demonstrated that, over the course of time, the expectation (the average growth over time) of those index returns is not only positive, but it is also greater than the returns offered by the majority of managed portfolios. This is because index returns are determined by the market as a whole.

It is far simpler to utter the phrase "set it and forget it" than it is to actually believe it and put it into practice. That is precisely why I decided to write the s that follow.

The Trading Of Options Explicated

Options, at their most fundamental level, are a sort of instrument that may be traded, in a manner that is comparable to that of more conventional types of securities such as stocks and bonds. When you buy an option, you are essentially buying a contract that grants you the right to either buy or sell a particular kind of asset at a specified price for a specific amount of time. This right is granted for the duration of the contract. This may appear to be a hard process; nevertheless, in reality, it is very similar to the one that has been experienced by anyone who has ever acquired a property with the assistance of a loan.

In this scenario, the buyer and the seller come to an agreement regarding the price of the house, and after that, the price of the house is confirmed. This occurs even if it takes some time for the buyer to complete the steps necessary to secure a loan from the bank. In the interim, the housing market could shift in such a way that the price of the home has greatly climbed, which would be beneficial for the buyer; alternatively, the price of the home could significantly decline, at which point the buyer could choose to withdraw their offer; this would be undesirable for the buyer. The buyer is protected in either case by the contract (or option), which ensures that they will obtain a certain bargain regardless of what transpires between the time that the contract is agreed upon and the date that it will expire.

There are many distinct forms of options; however, this guide will concentrate primarily on stock options. These options may be divided into two basic groups: those that are calls and those that are puts. Although there are many distinct types of options, this guide will primarily focus on stock options.

Calls are used to describe the activity of intending to buy a particular option, and this course of action is known as a call. If you decide to call an option, it is because you are operating under the presumption that the value of the underlying stock that is associated with that option will rise prior to the time when your call option will expire, allowing you to sell the stock at a profit. When you put your firm stock options into action, you are referred to as "calling" those options.

When you sell a particular stock at a particular price, you are establishing a put option instead of just selling the stock. Because you will only be able to make money if the stock whose option you are selling goes down in price significantly before it expires, the way you make money in this scenario depends on your hope that the stock will. Those who currently hold shares of a risky stock will frequently employ put options to safeguard the primary investment they have made in the stock. Because of the greater number of ways in which they differ from one another, exotic options should not be considered until after you have been familiar with everything that vanilla alternatives have to offer.

In addition, there are a few extra broad categories that each and every option, regardless of whether it is a put or a call, also fits into. The following are examples of what are known as "vanilla" options, which are examples of configurations that are likely to be encountered the most frequently.

Options that can be exercised at any moment before to the option's expiration time are referred to as American options, regardless of their country of origin. An option is deemed to be an American option if it may be done so.

European options: An option is referred to as having European characteristics if, regardless of where it was originated, it can only be exercised at the precise moment when it will no longer be available for use.

The term "short option" refers to any option that has an expiration date that is measured in terms of minutes, hours, or days.

Long options are those that do not expire for at least one year, which means that they are better suited for long term investing as opposed to day-to-day trading. Long options are also known as in-the-money options. Long options, also known as long equity anticipation securities (LEAPS), are another name for these financial instruments.

In addition, persons who engage in active trading of options can be divided into four distinct types. Holders are defined as individuals who purchase options, whereas writers are individuals who sell options. After that, holders and writers are classified further according to whether they work predominantly in calls or predominantly in puts. Holders have more power than authors do since holders have the option to either utilize an option to buy the connected stock in question or to let the time run out on the option if the market doesn't move in the way that they expected it to. authors, on the other hand, only have the option to sell the option. Writers, on the other hand, have their options constrained by the decisions made by the proprietor of the relevant intellectual property rights.

The Jargon of Options

The amount of obscure sounding jargon that the average options trader can spew in about 30 seconds can make the process more scary than it ultimately needs to be. However, there is nothing going on in an options exchange that is all that opaque. If you do yourself a favor and familiarize yourself with the following words and phrases, you will be well on your way to sounding like a professional, or at the at least, you will not become lost in their talks. So do yourself a favor and read on.

striking price: The striking price is the starting price of the stock that you are buying the option to buy or sell depending on whether you are generating a call or a put option. This varies based on which option you are creating.

Exercise: If the market moves in such a way that the amount of your striking price sounds appealing and you wish to sell or purchase the stock at the price in question, then you are said to be exercising the option. Exercise occurs when the market moves in such a way that the amount of your strike price sounds appealing.

Trading out: If you, as the option's holder, decide to sell the option, the option's writer will be able to buy it back through a procedure known as trading out. Trading out occurs when you agree to sell the option. This is the conclusion reached in more than fifty percent of all option deals. Only 10% of available alternatives are ever taken advantage of completely.

When referring to an option, something is considered to be "listed" if it is traded on a national exchange. Because listed options have clear strike prices and clear expiration dates, trading in them is an excellent area for beginners to begin their options trading careers. Listed options will almost certainly trade in blocks of 100 shares of the connected stock as its underlying asset.

The underlying stock of an option is the exact stock that the option is trading in. An option can only be traded in relation to the underlying stock.

On the right track: If the price of the underlying stock increases above the stock price throughout the time period of the call option, then the option is considered to be "in the money."

When a call option is "in the money," the difference in price between the current price and the strike price is referred to as the call option's "intrinsic value."

A single option's time value can be determined by determining how much time remains until the choice becomes invalid.

It is said to have a high level of volatility when the underlying stock that is associated with a particular option is prone to large variations in price with little to no prior warning. This is the definition of volatility.

Premium: The overall cost of the option in question, which takes into account the stock price, the strike price, the time value, and the volatility of the underlying asset.

Putting Together Your Strategy

The question now is, how exactly should one go about formulating a strategy? A comprehensive response is unquestionably warranted in light of the quality of this question. The first step in making a profitable trade is doing adequate research, and the second is formulating a detailed game plan. According to a well-known proverb, "failure to plan is planning to fail." After all, a strategy is just a comprehensive and well-thought-out plan, and if you are just starting out in the world of business, it is in your best interest to understand the steps you can take to develop a strategy that will ideally bring you a healthy profit.

Just Before You Get Started

It is highly recommended that you engage in "paper trading" first before moving on to actual trading. When you first begin, you will find that it is helpful to have a set of guidelines and procedures to follow, and the same is true when you practice here. In addition to this, it is a simple strategy that is also a practical way for you to understand the ins and outs of trading without having to spend any money on it. Sincerity requires me to tell you that there is not a single drawback to a paper trade that could possibly outweigh the benefits that a simulation actually brings to the table. Especially when you consider that it can assist prepare you and allow you to iron out many mistakes without having to suffer significant losses like many individuals do when they first start trading, which is bound to be the case for many people who start trading directly.

When you first begin your paper trade, it is in your best interest to select your goals and then either write them down or type them (if that is more your style). You are not simply trading and putting your money at risk for the sake of entertainment; you have certain aims in mind. In addition, you are going to need to write them down and commit them to memory in order to be able to remember them and adhere to them within a predetermined amount of time. It is the biggest lie you can tell someone that you will remember them even if you say you do not need to write them down because it is exceedingly unlikely that you will remember them. Writing down where you want to go and what you want to accomplish may really help you restrict the road you want to follow and give you a better picture of the goals you want to achieve. This is especially helpful if you are unsure of the path you want to take and are writing it down. Taking the time to write out your trading goals before engaging in penny stock trading is going to pay off in a big way, so don't be afraid to bring a pen and notebook with you, or even a tablet computer. Whatever makes you happy, you do you!

After that, you will have to decide which types or formats of penny stocks are most appealing to you. It is best to have familiarized yourself with the marketplaces you want to trade upon and to find a specialty that you are interested in and driven to work in. This will maximize your chances of being successful. It is a good idea to be familiar with the price range of the shares and the industry groupings whose products and services you like. When looking up those particular penny stock markets, don't forget to set any other parameters that you might have discovered to be significant.

The next phase is for you to determine the actions that you will do in terms of conducting research, maintaining monitoring, and trading shares. When you first get started, it will most likely be a really exciting time, but you must first determine where you will start. Which websites do you consider to be reliable? Will you get in touch with the company over the phone? Which of these reports do you plan to look into further? Do you have a complete understanding of all the material that is offered? Would you rather obtain the assistance and opinions of professionals? Which information sources will provide you the best details that you require at the end of the day? Those are the questions we want answered.

If you do not already have a broker, the selection of one is the next step that you will absolutely need to take. This becomes clear once you have achieved a level of comfort with the paper trading, and once you have amassed enough experience to be prepared to go on to the next major stage. Make it a point to get a trustworthy stockbroker who can cater to your individual requirements and preferences.

So there you have it! When getting started with penny stocks, there are seven steps and ideas that you should follow. In the end, it's not that difficult, but putting it all together will require a considerable lot of your time and energy. However, once you get things started, you should anticipate a significantly quicker speed for the remainder of the process.

When you are ready to begin searching for penny stocks to trade, there are a few things you need to keep in mind before you begin your search, including the following:

First, you should do some research on the company. Being a knowledgeable trader automatically qualifies one as a shrewd trader, thus this is a no-brainer. Doing a quick search on Google is the most effective method to get started with this, but doing so will almost likely not supply you with all of the information that you require. However, it can assist you in sorting through the worst stocks and determining whether or not the stock in question is worth devoting further time to researching.

When conducting research on stocks, it is imperative that you pay attention to the news tabs on Google Search. This is a feature that is sometimes disregarded, despite the fact that it is essential and may even be helpful. Taking into consideration the fact that there are more informative news stories regarding the stock in issue than there are blog postings.

After that, you will want to look at the volatility that is under consideration. When it comes to penny stocks, you are not searching for stocks that are not volatile, despite the fact that this may sound like an ironic statement to make. You should instead focus on working with equities that are climbing at a fairly quick rate instead. These are the companies that often have the biggest trading volume, and as a result, provide the most potential for making a profit (but also the greatest potential for losing money). You will have more than enough software at your disposal in today's current times to assist you in filtering the penny stocks that you are looking for. Consider it in this way if you're having trouble understanding why this is the case: when it comes to penny stocks, the less volatility that occurs during a trade, the fewer buyers and sellers there are. This indicates that you may have a significant amount of difficulty selling your shares and maintaining overall liquidity.

When it comes to investing in tiny stocks, volatility in penny stocks is beneficial and can put you light years ahead of the competition.

The second thing that you need to look at is the volume of the trade that is currently taking place. Although it is not the only aspect that can indicate whether or not a stock is a smart purchase, volatility is one of the factors that helps determine this. If a company does not have a lot of volume, then you should not even contemplate trading in it, regardless of how promising the company appears to be.

Trading volumes that run less than 200,000 shares a day are on the edge, and if you want to err on the side of caution, look for equities that trade less than 500,000 shares a day. A high volume of trades is an indication that there is a significant degree of interest being shown in the stocks. That indicates that if you make the decision to sell, you won't have a hard time finding a buyer and that the level of liquidity that already exists in that company won't or shouldn't be difficult to access. If you make the decision to sell.

Your attention should then be directed toward the catalysts. The basic function of a catalyst is to act as a predictor of a significant event that is taking place, more especially of news that can have an effect on or move a stock price regardless of whether the effect would be positive or negative.

For instance, if a firm is getting ready to launch a completely new and exciting project, you will be able to discover it on the catalyst and maybe anticipate that it will have a good impact on the company; this, of course, is predicated on the success of the product.

When you are thinking about investing in a stock, it is always a good idea to have a quick look at the catalyst and observe how exactly it is that they are moving the stock prices. You might even have a clearer understanding of what to keep an eye out for and acquire a handle on the trends that have an effect on stock prices.

It is beneficial to take into consideration the viewpoints of others. It does not imply that you should always follow their recommendations, but having a grasp of the ideas and viewpoints of others can provide you with an advantage over other people. It is a good idea to examine what people say about penny stocks, even on social media; however, you should always take what they say about penny stocks with a grain of salt. This piece of advise does come with a warning. This should only serve as a type of study, and your ultimate and final decision should not be influenced in any way by it until it can be confirmed by other facts and actual credible sources. Having said that, the best thing you can do for yourself in the long run is to train your mind to think independently. Initially, you will do this by watching the behaviors of other people and determining for yourself whether or not their moves are correct. You are not simply replicating what they are doing; rather, you are learning how to apply certain situations in your favor while dismissing the choices of others that will not work in your scenario. In other words, you are learning how to apply certain conditions in your favor rather than simply copying what they are doing.

Similar to the sensation that one gets when they have déjà vu, history has a tendency to repeat itself, although not exactly in the same way each time. However, becoming familiar with the patterns of penny stocks can provide you with a relatively solid understanding regarding the possible outcomes of various penny stocks. It's possible that you should conduct your trading based on the same key patterns that keep appearing again and over. Although it could be a little tedious at times, it is quite dependable. And because you are just starting off, you should think about using this technique until you become familiar with other types of methods, or you should simply continue using it if it is successful. You have complete control over that aspect.

When it comes to trading, the time of day is an important factor to take into consideration. It is easy to misjudge the passage of time when one leads a hectic lifestyle. When it comes to trading, though, it is essential to remain aware of what is taking place in the market. If you also have another job, the most convenient trading schedule for you will be one that fits around your other obligations. If you are a student, for instance, you can devote the morning to studying and going to classes, and the afternoon to trading; alternatively, you can do it the other way around if it works better with your schedule.

The trading strategy that you decide to implement may need to be adjusted depending on the time of day that you do most of your work. For instance, working on particular stocks in the morning can be quite profitable, but those same equities might end up with a loss after the market has closed for the day. In situations like these, picking up patterns and modifying them to fit your needs in terms of time and resources can be very helpful.

Steer clear of investing in businesses that have enormous amounts of outstanding debt. Any corporation that is carrying a significant amount of debt is a giant red flag that should be waving from a tall tower. Therefore, when researching a company that trades in penny stocks, it is essential to have a comprehensive understanding of the firm as a whole, which unquestionably include the state of the company's finances on an aggregate level.

To get at this conclusion, it is recommended that one utilize the technical type of analysis; nevertheless, one should also take into account the essential accounts. Spend some quality time reading the reports in order to have an accurate understanding of what is going on within the organization. This is typically a reliable sign of the state of the firm, and if you notice that the company is in over its head with debt, it is quite unlikely that it will be successful. Does this indicate that you are unable to engage in trade? You certainly can, but you'll need to make some adjustments to your plan and bear in mind that the amount of debt will have a significant impact on the stocks. As a direct consequence of this, there is a greater possibility that you will incur a loss.

You should keep an eye out for penny stocks that do have greater and more favorable ratios in their liquidity. This is something you should be looking for. When you compare a company's assets to its debts, you can calculate its liquidity ratio from the result. Every business has its share of assets and debts. If the ratio of the firm's assets to its liabilities is more than one, then the company is in a better financial position because this is a vital indicator that the company's capital outweighs its liabilities. This indicates that the company is operating pretty effectively at the present moment and that there is potential for the company to take action in the future.

The next step is for you to consider using a stock screener, which will assist you in reducing the number of options available to you by employing the criteria that you have previously established. In addition to this, it gives you the ability to search for a greater number of factors, such as volume, volatility, and so on.

Problems Presented By Technology

While it's possible that peer-to-peer file sharing worked well for reusable content like music, articles, and photographs, it cannot function as an electronic alternative for currency or any other kind of so-called "exchange of value." If the sender or contributor to a decentralized database is indifferent to the value of the content, then they are also indifferent to the number of exact clones of a file that exist at any given time or continue to be made. This is because the value of the material is not something that can be controlled by the sender or contributor. (This is what disturbed the actual owners of content on music file sharing websites, as well as the artists and their respective music corporations, who ultimately succeeded in closing down the peer-to-peer file sharing website Napster). On a peer-to-peer network whose objective was to exist beyond the purview of central authorities, this created a unique challenge: how to send files over the network, while having the total supply of such files restricted, the provenance verified, and the privacy of users maintained - in a system highly decentralized. In the case of a currency where the supply and record of ownership (i.e. provenance) is of the utmost importance, file redundancy and replication must be tightly controlled. In spite of contributions from well-qualified and respected figures like Hal Finney, Adam Back (of Hashcash fame), Nick Szabo, and Wei Dai, the efforts of the cypherpunks community for many years had failed to create such a system. This was due to the difficulty of the challenge, which was one reason why Wei Dai's "b-money" is one notable example because of its similarity to Bitcoin in its use of encryption.

With this in mind, we will heavily cite from the Bitcoin whitepaper that was published on October 31, 2008, so the reader can learn from the actual words of Satoshi Nakamoto how the challenge was to be addressed by utilizing the tools we learned about in 2, while adding a game-theoretic mining competition to allow for decentralized transaction validation. The reader can learn from the actual words of Satoshi Nakamoto because we will heavily cite from the Bitcoin whitepaper. At a variety of points throughout the text, we will enter our own thoughts into "Authors' Note" boxes that are formatted with italics and shading.

Who Will Fill the Metaverse? is the Topic of 5.

People will inhabit the Metaverse through digital representations known as avatars. In the Metaverse, each of us takes on the form of a distinct person. It is quite unlikely that your behavior offline and online will be identical to one another. The version of yourself that you present online and the one that you actually are are almost always two distinct things. These numerous incarnations of you use a variety of spellings of your name, and you probably don't use the same level of formality in your online interactions that you do in the office. There are a variety of avatars you can use to represent yourself online.

In the Metaverse, we can construct new identities for ourselves known as Avatars.

What exactly does the term avatar mean?

A picture of a Sims character or an image that seems like a cartoon is comparable to the avatar, and there are other photos of the avatar that are deeper and more reflective of the character.

The NFT will be used to build digital profile photos that feature a character with characteristics that have been generated randomly by the algorithm. These characteristics will be included in the digital profile photographs. Our one-of-a-kind representations in the Metaverse are called NFTs, and they serve as our avatars. The NTFS presents genuine examples of digital art. You have the ability to take ownership of your avatar, making you both easily identifiable and one-of-a-kind inside the Metaverse. You have the option of purchasing the sole ownership of the commercial use of the avatar. You can even earn digital currency such as cryptocurrency if you work hard enough. It is possible to demonstrate that you have a high status in Metaverse by demonstrating that you are an expert in cryptography. You can portray yourself for a certain task as a mythological or perfect version of who you are or who you would like it to become. Alternatively, you can present yourself as a version of who you would like it to become.

In the Metaverse, one's digital identity has replaced their avatar. Since we were young, the internet has played a significant role in the development of our characters. When we make a new application or game app, we start from scratch and give it a brand new persona each time. Over the past twenty years, everyone has developed an online identity for themselves. Lots of people have become popular on Instagram, TikTok, funny memes, and so on. However, when you actually come face to face with these famous people, you most likely won't even recognize them. They are not the same in almost every way, despite how they present themselves to the world.

Through the usage of the Metaverse, we are able to construct a permanent identity for ourselves, one that may be utilized in any environment. Metaverse lets us have a unique identity and frees us to be who we are, and we are free from real-life day-to-day activities. You can be successful in endeavors that would be impossible in the actual world. In the real world, developing your profession, business, or brand might take a significant amount of time, but in the metaverse, this is something that can be accomplished with relative ease.

When a brand is destroyed in real life, the damage to your image may be permanent; however, the Metaverse gives you the opportunity to start again and create a new identity.

The Avatar

When attempting to communicate with other users in virtual reality, it is necessary to use an avatar. A significant number of Facebook's applications will soon be updated to support virtual reality avatars. As Facebook prepares to launch the Metaverse, these modifications will begin to set the groundwork for social virtual reality on the platform. The avatar is capable of reacting to the movement of the player's body, moving around, touching things, and carrying on a dialogue using both their mouth and facial expressions. The new avatar on Facebook is compatible with about three updated applications on Facebook that are available in the Oculus store. These applications are Epic roller coasters, Topgolf with the pro putt, and PokerStars VR. The Metaverse is the most comprehensive app, and it is expected to contain the most of the Avatars functionality.

Because it will be utilized in the Metaverse, which represents a transition from playing a game to actually having a social existence, the avatar is of utmost significance. The Avatars are fungible non-tokens that can be used within the Oculus VR. The newer avatars feature a variety of bodies and faces, each of which is more detailed than before. You have the option of selecting the one who wears unusual clothing or has piercings. Avatars are similar to humans; however, rather of having unremarkable hair, eyes, and noses, as well as jewelry, they now have more elaborate versions of these features. Everyone now has the ability to give an accurate representation of themselves thanks to their new avatar.

Having an Understanding of the Opposite

There are a few topics of conversation that need to be covered first, and then we can go on to the subject of passive funds. You have an obligation to gain an understanding of these ideas because they will be your competitors during the process of investing and even hurdles that you have to surmount. Your financial portfolio will be ruined if you do not take the time to comprehend these ideas and make enough preparations for them. We are going to go through each of these things in turn.

The rate of inflation

In the field of economics, this term refers to a measurement that identifies the rate at which the general price level of particular commodities and services rises over the course of a specific amount of time. In a nutshell, following the passage of a predetermined amount of time, a predetermined sum of currency will become less valued in the market. For instance, in the year 1990, twenty dollars could purchase a particular quantity of apples. However, as a result of inflation over time, the value of apples rises up, which means that twenty dollars will only buy you a smaller quantity of apples.

When people of a more senior generation talk about how a specific amount of money used to be equivalent to being rich in the past, this idea is sometimes trivialized and poked fun at in a humorous manner. When I was younger, fifty cents was a significant amount of money. How many times have we already encountered this expression? As you've gotten older, the costs of many things that are essential to your life have gone up, whether it be gasoline, food, automobiles, land, real estate, or entertainment. A higher rate of inflation signified a decline in the purchasing power of a country's currency.

When a currency's purchasing power decreases due to inflation, the cost of living for the general population as a whole goes up by a sizeable amount. The decline in consumers' ability to make purchases as a result of all of this activity causes a significant deceleration in the rate of economic expansion. The vast majority of economists are of the opinion that inflation develops when there is a barrier posed by a nation's money supply to economic expansion. The primary monetary authority of a nation undertakes whatever has to be done to ensure that inflation does not spiral out of control and to ensure that the economy continues to function normally. The monetary authority can be compared to a central bank to some extent. These firms have access to a variety of tools that can help them maintain everything within the appropriate parameters.

There are many different factors that contribute to inflation. The cause of this problem is the general trend of increasing costs. There are three distinct categories that can be used to describe the causes of inflation.

The demand-pull effect is a form of inflation that takes place when the demand for specific goods and services significantly exceeds the capacity of the economy to produce them. The circumstance of strong demand and insufficient supply leads to the inevitable outcome of increased prices for the product or service in question. For instance, if a single automaker decides to cut back on the quantity of automobiles it manufactures, this will result in a lower supply. A supply-demand gap will be created if the demand remains constant or increases, and the manufacturer will have no choice but to raise prices as a result of the public's desire for the automobile, which will ultimately result in inflation.

The cost-push effect is the consequence of higher prices incurred all throughout the production process. The price of the finished product or service may go up as a direct result of several factors, such as an increase in the cost of labor or an increase in the price of raw materials. For instance, the rise in the price of raw materials such as wood, glass, and cement could cause a significant increase in the cost of housing.

Inflation that is built in occurs when the price of products and services rises because workers anticipate and want greater salaries at the same time. This is done to ensure that the expense of living does not fall behind the rate of inflation. The higher earnings that follow from these pay increases cause further rises in the cost of products and services, and the cycle continues from this point on.

With very limited exceptions, inflation is a problem that will never be solved. costs of products and services as a whole will not be comparable to what they were fifty years ago, and costs fifty years from now will be significantly higher than they are right now. The rate of inflation can be brought under control by the application of a variety of different monetary policy instruments. However, these are mostly beyond the ability of the common person to influence, and the responsibility for addressing them typically rests on the shoulders of financial regulars such as the central bank.

When viewed from the perspective of the person, inflation can either be good or damaging to the economy. People who have assets such as stocks or investment properties would likely benefit from inflation because the value of those assets will go up as a result of the increase in inflation. Inflation is likely to be unpopular among those who have financial goals including the acquisition of investments or the maintenance of cash reserves because it will require them to spend more money. The trick is to keep inflation at the ideal level while at the same time preventing it from spiraling out of control. In this approach, purchasers will have an improved sense of spending confidence, while investors will continue to witness an increase in the value of their portfolios.

Even if you may not have any influence over inflation, this does not mean that you are unable to take any action to manage it. You can protect your investments and savings by engaging in specific activities; doing so will ensure that you do not lose all of your money. The best defense your money can have against the effects of inflation is a diversified investment portfolio. Diversification, on the other hand, does not ensure protection against the loss of funds, nor does it guarantee profits on investments.

Investments known as Inflation-protected Securities, or IPS, have a rate of return that is adjusted for inflation, which ensures that investors will receive a return on their money in the long run. Treasury Inflation-Protected Securities and Corporate Inflation-Protected Securities are both examples of IPS investments. The former are issued by the federal government, and the latter are issued by corporations operating in the private sector.

Investing in stocks is another way to protect your money from the effects of inflation. The rise in the cost of living is typically accompanied by an increase in stock prices. If you are currently hanging onto a stock and inflation takes place, the value of your holdings has increased due to the rising cost of living.

About what inflation is and how it might effect various people in different ways, we could write books all day long. When you first start becoming involved in the world of investments, one thing that you absolutely cannot overlook is inflation. That is the primary objective of this section. The more you comprehend it, the more you will be able to utilize it to your benefit. If you fail to keep an eye on inflation and the kinds of problems it might cause, you will almost certainly find yourself in a position where you cannot prevail.

There Are Two Varieties Of Stock Analysis

The fundamental analysis and the technical analysis of stocks are going to be covered in this section so that you may learn how to conduct both of them.

Analysis of the Fundamentals

The value of a stock is determined with the help of concrete information (i.e., the performance of the company) while conducting this kind of study. As the name suggests, it makes use of fundamental facts about the company, such as its marketability, profitability, and competitive edge, among other things. Investors will utilize the information provided here to determine the true value of a company. People that use fundamental analysis concentrate on the financial statements of the company (such as the balance sheet, income statement, cash flow statements, and so on). Fundamental analysis places a significant emphasis on these data since they provide insight into both the past and present performance of an organization.

Analysis on a Technical Level

In a broad sense, the purpose of this kind of analysis is to investigate the financial market in and of itself. Technical analysts evaluate the value of a stock not by using information linked to a company, but rather by analyzing economic aspects (such as the current price, product volume, supply and demand factors, etc.). This is done in place of utilizing information relating to a company.

Workplace Photos of Stock Analysts (Source: www.flickr.com)

The Stock Market's Foundational Investing Principles and Strategies

Buy and Hold Stocks That Have Been Carefully Selected - Trading stocks, which involves buying and selling shares of a company in the hope of making a rapid profit, is a high-risk approach, particularly for investors with little to no prior experience. In order to forecast future price fluctuations, this method analyzes market trends and performs complex mathematical calculations. To summarize, stock traders are subject to a greater number of dangers than stock investors are. When you make transactions with your broker, you are subject to certain fees and taxes, and we need to take those into consideration as well.

On the other side, you can reduce the amount of risk that you have to incur by purchasing and holding on to the stocks that you have selected. Using this method, you will have an easier time overcoming fluctuating prices and avoiding paying exorbitant transaction fees.

Invest in Mutual Funds – According to professionals in the financial industry, novice investors should concentrate on low-cost no-load mutual funds (especially those that purchase the entire stock market). A minimum initial commitment of between $2,500 and $5,000 is necessary to open an account with virtually every company that manages mutual funds. Fidelity, Charles Schwab, and Vanguard are currently three of the most well-known and respected companies in the mutual fund industry.

Utilize a strategy known as dollar-cost averaging. This method involves purchasing the same dollar amount of a stock on a predetermined timetable at regular intervals. For instance, if you intend to invest $2,000 in a certain business, you might buy $500 worth of shares from that business once a month for a period of four months. This frees you from the need to carefully time the purchase of stocks in the future. Your purchases, on average, will cost you a "just" amount, which will be reflected in the total cost of those purchases.

Statements Of Financial Position

It is not always a good thing to have access to an excessive amount of information, and let's face it: there is so much information that you are likely to be left feeling bewildered as a result. In light of this, it is important that you, as a value investor, pay attention to financial statements. They provide you with information regarding the source of the money as well as the destination of the funds. In other words, they serve as an excellent predictor of how well a company is performing, and you can make your decision regarding whether or not to invest based on what you learn from them. The problem with these assertions is that they can be somewhat challenging for someone who is just starting out to comprehend. The purpose of this is to demystify financial statements and make them easier to understand.

Concerns Relating to Accounting

Accounting should be important to you if you are a value investor since it gives you an accurate depiction of the company's financial situation that you are analyzing. When it comes to accounting, there is a considerable amount of leeway that may be taken into consideration when calculating income, costs, and the value of assets. It is necessary to have the ability to read between the lines of a financial statement because a large number of businesses naturally take advantage of the flexibility that is afforded to them. You do not require all of the information that can be provided in a statement. You need only focus on the aspects of the situation that are relevant. Now that we've covered the basics, let's talk about the different kinds of financial statements you can acquire.

Both the 10-K Annual Report and the 10-Q Quarterly Report can be found here.

The value investor cannot function without these reports in any capacity. The Securities and Exchange Commission (SEC) ensures that financial reports from corporations are consistent, accurate, reported often, and easily accessible. As a result, we are in possession of these reports. A 10-K report will provide you with a comprehensive summary of the company, including information on its assets, technologies, personnel numbers, client base, and patents.

You will also receive information regarding the company's markets, such as the position, size, growth, share, strengths, threats, and competition in those markets; in-depth financials with up to five or 10 years of research, as well as notes to clarify what the data all represent; and information regarding the company's products and services.

You will receive explanations of pensions, acquisitions, other key transactions, risk factors, and how the company's performance might be influenced by them, as well as an analysis of the company's financial condition, its results, and its prospects moving forward from management. Last but not least, you are provided with a detailed account of any legal actions in which the company might be engaged.

These reports contain a variety of sections, including but not limited to the following:

• Highlights demonstrating the most significant financial results in terms of earnings, sales, and productivity, often over a period of five years.

• A letter to shareholders describing the previous year and the upcoming year, milestones attained, and new ones to accomplish. This letter is often written by the CEO and is addressed to shareholders.

• A synopsis of the company's operations, which will include a discussion of all of the information that is essential to your understanding of the company's goods, its markets, and its rivals. You will also gain knowledge regarding patents, seasonality, and any overseas exposure, all of which may have some bearing on the firm. This accounts for the dangers that the company is exposed to as well.

• An review of the company's finances, including sales, expenses, costs, liabilities, assets, liquidity, and risks associated with expanding into new markets.

• A number of statements of finances that have been integrated. "Consolidated," in the sense that the assertions have been written in a manner that is both quick to read and simple to comprehend. You'll discover the balance sheet, which is often referred to as the statement of financial situation or position, in these documents. This provides an overview of the company's liabilities, assets, and equity at a specific point in time, indicating the company's current financial status. The income statement, which is also known as the operating activity statement or the statement of operations, details the financial performance of the company during a specified time period. This performance is broken down into several categories, including sales, costs of sales, expenses, and the variance between costs and sales. Last but not least, you will receive a statement of cash flows, which summarizes, in monetary terms, the performance and activities of the organization over a predetermined period of time. Cash-flows tell you about cash or checks that come in or go out of a firm, which enables you to determine how liquid a company is and whether or not the earnings shown on the statement are legitimate or faked. • Cash-flows let you know about cash or checks that come in or go out of a business. In addition to the financial statements, some ones of these reports will also include something called a common size statement. These common size statements are essentially the same as financial statements; however, they are presented in percentage form, which makes it much simpler for you to compare different businesses. comments are also provided in the report. These comments might provide you with information that you might overlook if you just looked at the numbers. For example, they can inform you about how the firm accounts for options, the techniques it uses for depreciation, the financing it provides for pensions, and other similar topics. In addition to that, it may encompass things like the closing of enterprises, mergers and acquisitions, as well as alterations to the systems of accounting.

• The review that was conducted by the auditor is included in the report, and it can typically be found somewhere in the back. The purpose of the review is to lend credibility to the procedures that the firm uses for its finances and accounting. Keep an eye out for critiques that are more extensive than three pages in length. If you come across the phrases "adverse" or "qualified" in the third paragraph, you should proceed with caution regarding that organization.

Replicating The Success Of Their Investments

The use of index funds

A number of years back, Warren Buffett placed a wager against the administrators of a significant hedge fund. The hedge fund's area of expertise was managing the investments of its clients and monitoring the growth of those investments. Warren Buffett held a contrary viewpoint, namely that it did not matter how skilled an investor was, they would never be able to generate as much revenue from the stock market as they could if they placed their money in an index fund. The wager was made over a ten-year period, and the winner would get one million dollars. The prize money was primarily used for symbolic purposes because all of the parties participating already had tens of millions of dollars, if not billions of dollars like Buffett himself. However, the bet was significant because it represented an essential concept: could investors truly outplay the market as a whole?

This wager was placed on the premise that investing in index funds is an all-around safer bet than making an effort to outperform the average performance of the market. An index fund is a type of mutual fund in which the total amount of money held by the fund grows in proportion to the overall performance of an exchange. You may, for instance, place your money in an index fund that is affiliated with the New York Stock Exchange; in this case, the fund's value will increase provided that the exchange as a whole is thriving. There was no doubt over whether or not the value of the fund would increase, but the question that remained was whether or not the fund could truly outrun one of the most competitive hedge funds in the world. Surprisingly, the answer was that index funds truly do have the potential to outperform even the most knowledgeable investors in the world. Investors, as a group, had committed a serious error in judgment when they attempted to outperform the market as a whole by placing their wagers on certain businesses while ignoring those of others. This gamble demonstrates that it does not matter how intelligent or talented an investor is; an index fund will always outperform the bets that the investor makes. In addition, there is zero effort required to monitor the performance of an index fund. You simply hand over your money and watch it grow in value; you are not required to switch around investments, nor are you required to select companies that you believe will do better than the market average.

Index funds can have some limitations, especially for individuals with a smaller amount of capital to invest. If you invest in an index fund, you shouldn't expect to begin seeing returns on your investment for approximately four to five years after making the investment. This is the normal amount of time that you should plan on having your money invested for. You are free to withdraw the interest at predetermined intervals; however, it is generally recommended that you leave the money invested in the fund so that the fund can expand at a more rapid pace. I would recommend this path to any investor who is comfortable with making an investment that will be held for a period of five years. Investing as much money as you possibly can in an index fund is the best way to ensure that you get the most out of this type of investment. Nevertheless, this is one of the most risk-free investments that you could possibly make, and putting your money in a fund for a period of five years poses an exceptionally minimal risk.

There are two key risks associated with index funds, however even taking into account just one of these challenges can still result in significant financial gain for an investor. There are two primary concerns: first, that the stock market would suffer a crash from which it will be unable to recover, and second, that the stock market will participate in a worldwide recession, which will result in inflation that is higher than the growth of the index fund. The first possible outcome of a worldwide catastrophe is extremely improbable, and the government has demonstrated that it will do all within its power to prevent a total breakdown of the global financial system. If this hypothetical future comes to pass, you will have a great deal more to worry about than just the money you have in your investment fund. Because of this, no investment can be considered absolutely safe because a large-scale crash that might wipe out an index fund would probably also take a major section of the US economy with it. The second possibility, which is that the economy will enter a recession, should not cause nearly as much concern as the first one. Buffett was able to emerge victorious in the wager that he placed with the managers of the hedge funds despite the severity of the economic downturn that occurred at the turn of the previous decade. What this means for a typical investor is that after five years, there is a possibility that they will have lost some money, but after ten years, they will have earned back any money they lost plus additional profits. Even if it is conceivable for an index fund to incur losses over a certain time period, those losses will not persist for the course of the fund's entire existence. This indicates that if you discover that the value of your fund has truly decreased, you can continue to invest your money in the fund for an extended period of time, until the value of the fund increases beyond the level at which it began and you begin to generate returns that are meaningful again. The fact that you will have less access to your money for a longer period of time is the main disadvantage of this option. I would recommend this strategy of investment to anyone who possesses an investment fund of a respectable size, but I would warn them that they should prepare themselves for the possibility that they won't be able to access their money for at least five years, and that this doesn't even take into account the accrued interest; in the worst case scenario, the money won't be available for ten years. In either scenario, when you take the money out of the account, you will have earned a higher proportion of returns than you would have with any hedge fund. You always have the option to collect the interest as it accrues in order to generate immediate cash flow; however, it is possible that it will be more beneficial to do so once you have allowed the fund to mature for a few years.

AKA: "mutual funds"

Following the purchase of an index fund, the next investment vehicle that you should consider is a mutual fund. A mutual fund is a type of organization that pools the funds contributed by individual investors and invests them collectively in groups of equities that are generally regarded as being secure investments. You have learned in two that there are stocks that pay dividends in order to entice investors and maintain their investment in the stock. These are the kinds of companies that mutual funds invest in; they are stocks that have a history of making consistent payouts at predetermined intervals and that are also very stable. A mutual fund may also diversify its holdings by investing in assets other than stocks, such as treasury bonds and even stock options, in addition to stock holdings. They will not stop at anything short of achieving a satisfactory rate of return for their backers.

Mutual funds are vital for generating a quick flow of cash, despite the fact that they might not generate as much interest over the long term as an index fund does. This is one of the nice things about mutual funds. You are free to withdraw any portion of your investment in a mutual fund at any time without incurring any penalties, with the exception that the amount you withdraw will be considered taxable income for the year in which it is received. A mutual fund is required to provide its investors with regular updates on the status of their accounts.

When I first started investing, mutual funds were an important component in building up an early income stream for my portfolio. I invested a total of $3,000 in a mutual fund offered by T. Rowe

Price, and after a period of one year, the fund generated returns of approximately $200. Rather than withdrawing the principal investment from the mutual fund, I would take the interest instead. It is obvious that leaving the money in the mutual fund would have resulted in more benefits in the long run; but, that was not the purpose of this transaction; rather, it was to ensure that I would be able to collect immediate cash flow from my investment.

I would recommend that you start investing with a mutual fund, and that you open an account with somewhere around one thousand dollars to get things started. T. Rowe Price is an investment company that, based on my personal experience, I would recommend. They provide a number of mutual funds, each of which has a distinct amount of predicted risk. This means that you have the option of pursuing a high level of returns in a short period of time at the expense of a higher level of risk, or you may opt for a more secure position in exchange for lower returns. For my own part, I decided to go with the middle option of a fund, which was one that was somewhat risk-free but yet offered a respectable rate of anticipated return. I recommend taking this route if you want instant income, and using an index fund if you want to invest for a longer time period. You can discover the mutual fund that is appropriate for you with the projected returns that are most advantageous for the risk that you are willing to take on. You can find the mutual fund that is right for you with the expected returns that are most favorable for the risk that you are willing to take on.

The Path That Led Us Here

When I was in clinical school, I had no idea what a doctor's salary was. Even while I was aware that experts made good progress, I didn't have a solid understanding of the numbers until after

I graduated. In 1987, while I was conducting my muscle preparation at a clinic in Cincinnati, I was introduced to the public for the first time during a gathering.

When we were in the middle of our morning meeting, all of a sudden, we were startled by the sound of thunder that sounded like an earthquake. Since I was from Texas and had no idea whether or not Ohio had experienced earthquakes, I inquired as to the status of the situation. The more experienced physician was the one who drove the conversation, and he remarked, "Goodness, that is Dr. this and that with his new speedster." To be more specific, it was a twin-turbocharged Porsche 959 that was barely road legal, had to be specially arranged, and cost several times as much as my yearly resident wage! That gave me hope for the future in terms of my financial situation.

We are all aware that recent events have brought about some shifts. In the end, the costs of medical treatment came in higher than the expansion, and after that, they lost their power. As a direct result of this, physicians have been subjected to consistent monetary and administrative assaults.

Insurance companies have evolved into revenue-driven entities that squander every little bit they can get their hands on. The specialists are currently the most vulnerable connection in this clinical environment, and they are powerless to defend themselves against insurance companies, medical clinics, and large doctor associations that are governed by corporations. The amount that the doctor must repay each year decreases as a result of expansion. Concurrently, there is a natural progression toward an increase in costs associated with business growth. This increase in costs is made worse by requirements for excessive programming and the continually increasing amounts of representatives required to remain knowledgeable of unofficial laws and to manage protection forms.

Because of this edge compression, the company has decided to form a union. A significant number of medical practitioners are currently employed full-time by sizable organizations or urgent care centers. In theory, this should improve production; nevertheless, in practice, it is disrupting specialist patient connections and reducing compensations. It is not the physician who is treating the patient who is making the decisions; rather, organizations and sheets are making those decisions.

Because of this, there is an evident level of dissatisfaction associated with the medical profession. Some of the comments that I've read include the following: "You should simply feel warm and fluffy realizing that you helped humankind... ideally, not spending retirement living in a cardboard box under a scaffolding someplace." Another physician expressed their sorrow that "all that administrative work drains the happiness out of being a doctor."1 Physician burnout has reached an all-time high and currently hovers around the 50 percent mark.2 This indicates that some of the professionals out there have had to give up medication at one point in their lives, and it's possible that some of them still do. There are numerous different reasons why this emergency has occurred: breaking down student obligations, increasing administrative errands, such a huge number of hours spent working, challenging electronic healthcare records, declining repayments, and a lack of control and independence are some of the issues that have been brought up. Numerous medical professionals have considered leaving the field of medicine due to the extensive list of challenges they face. Some people have mentioned that they could desire to stay in the event that they discover a way to improve their circumstances.

When they decide to become doctors, most people give up the third decade of their lives to study and train for the profession. Because of the high expense of the education, many students are saddled with student loans that range from $150,000 to $200,000.3 THIS WILL IMMEDIATELY CAUSE FINANCIAL AND LIFESTYLE STRESS. I just had a conversation with a muscular specialist on the West Coast who expressed a debt of $400,000 from his training. That would take the majority of doctors a very long time to recoup their investment. My daughter has recently finished a pediatric residency in which she worked with 34 different doctors. Everyone had to fulfill credit commitments.

Not only are young doctors faced with massive amounts of debt, but when adjusted for inflation, physician reimbursement is either remaining the same or actually decreasing. These days, clinical understudies are paying more than they ever have before for their education, which comes at a time when they are joining a career in which the salary is decreasing.

Despite the fact that the earnings for doctors are stagnant, we are actually able to make a living that is above and beyond what was anticipated. Despite this, control is increasingly being ceded to more powerful narcotics. Specialists run the risk of becoming insignificant cogs in a massive, profit-driven medical machine if the framework doesn't undergo a dramatic shift in direction.

If we are unable to eradicate the challenging foundation and oversight that has led to the contamination of drugs over the course of the past few years, then we need to rethink our approach. You are fortunate in that you have the ability to accept responsibility for your own predetermination, and that is the subject of this book.

You will have more leeway and more command over how you practice medicine as a result of the fact that you will not be subject to specialist pay from drugs. This will create an atmosphere that is more endearing to your patients as well as one that allows them to concentrate more intently. You may continue to work within the same framework; but, you will have the opportunity to do away with or change conditions that adversely affect your time, your salary, and the attention and participation of your patients with the office.

Your life will evolve as you take responsibility for your professional and financial circumstances. Because of this, not only will your life and the life of your family improve, but the lives of your patients will also improve because you will be less stressed. Your opportunities, compassion, and sound reasoning will have a positive impact on the lives of individuals with whom you come in contact, and the ripple effect of this influence may help to make the world a better place. This is the primary motivation behind our desire for "rich doctors."

As you begin your exploration, there are two potential hazards that you should keep an eye out for:

1. The activity in which you engage the most. We are frequently indoctrinated to believe that arduous labor is the essential factor that contributes to achievement. It's possible that's true, but nobody's ever suggested you shouldn't be able to enjoy the scenery along the way. I have noticed that the more objectively I approach a subject, the greater my appreciation for that subject becomes. Why not modify that condition a little bit and let the things that you enjoy doing reveal the things that you are typically good at?

2. What makes the most effort to present itself to you. As you learn more about the area and conduct explorations, you could notice that certain kinds of opportunities present themselves to you

more frequently than others. Which land options appear to be resurfacing again and again in your thoughts? This is something that needs your attention.

As a direct result of the second reason I said, I had the opportunity to work out the details of what will go smoothly for me in terms of my contribution to the property. I had the distinct impression that rather than me choosing investment properties, those properties chose me. Up until that point, I had been researching and thinking about anything and everything except than investment homes, but suddenly they came up. They presented themselves to me in such a natural and effortless manner that I was given the opportunity to take action on them more quickly than I had ever anticipated, and I even started a business with them.

Do I have an appreciation for real estate investments? Indeed, and the answer is no. They are exactly what they appear to be. Finding new ones to buy and breaking down the numbers is something that I enjoy doing in my spare time. Because I hire a property manager to handle the day-to-day operations of my rental properties after I purchase them, I am typically not overly involved with them and I maintain a certain amount of emotional distance from them. My property manager is responsible for finding and screening potential tenants, taking maintenance requests, supervising workers who are hired, keeping up with legal and contractual obligations, and responding to emergencies. I will freely admit, though, that resolving concerns involving residents is not one of my favorite tasks, regardless of whether or not the property manager is responsible for doing so. However, I do enjoy the regular passive income that I receive from the homes each month, and I've found that my charging time has been even more enjoyable ever since I've owned investment properties owing to the added profits I get for the houses themselves. For me, however, they are really even more of a vehicle for what it is that I need, which is simple revenue, than they are something that I am too enthusiastic about. Nevertheless, I am not surprised by them.

I mentioned earlier that I had at least some motive to recognize that I wasn't actually effective at supervising people who were hired to do work for someone else. Because of the shelving, I was unknowingly naive while dealing with a project worker who took advantage of my trusting nature. In addition, I've had several interactions with excellent project employees, but despite this, I've realized on multiple occasions how little I enjoy managing people. This was validated a couple of years into my ownership of one of my investment properties when an occupant caused extensive smoke damage throughout the whole interior of the house, and I was required to get the home entirely rehabilitated after the damage was done. It was tough enough to manage the renovation process; I didn't even bother getting my hands filthy. I detested every single second of it, from the beginning, when the first project worker I had working on the house became completely obsessed with her work until the end, when I had to spend almost two weeks supervising the second project worker. It was not everyone's cup of tea to have to make multiple trips to Home Depot throughout the day, fight through constant traffic, watch the price counts ring up on the register, coordinate the participation of a number of different people in the finishing of the property, and repeatedly discover things that weren't done correctly.

What are rehabs? This time it won't work. In the event that ramming my face-first into a partition wouldn't have resulted in additional work for the person in charge of the project, I would have done it while I was trying to cope with the aftermath of that recuperation. I was given a wonderful piece of property in exchange, and I was given the opportunity to rent it out for far more money than I could have done before the recovery; nevertheless, I will never have to deal with another recovery again.

The basic issue is one of swimming against the current with regard to land contributions or with regard to everything else encountered in day-to-day life, worthy motivations leading to disappointment. I unquestionably believe that you will not be successful if you go against the grain of your typical behavior in the same way that you will be successful if you engage in activities that come naturally to you. It could take some time and effort on your part to figure out what you are good at and what interests you, but you should consider it part of the learning process.

If you stick to doing things in the way that comes most naturally to you, you will find that you have the most success. That entails achieving monetary success while having a pleasant experience while doing so, as well as creating advancement. Make every effort to avoid being the fish that swims against the current and tries to swim upstream. If you let your own stream carry you, you'll discover that contributing will be much simpler after you do so.

The Most Successful Approach To Day Trading

HFT is the most effective approach for day trading, especially for those just starting out. Mastering HFT is not very difficult. Because of this, High-Frequency Trading (HFT) is the most effective method for beginning investors. In addition to this, the amount of investment money that is required is not excessive. If you sign up for a discount account, you can multiply your initial investment of $500 into a sum that is at least somewhat respectable in a matter of weeks. Naturally, the more trades you engage in, the better the chances are that you will see an increase in your capital.

You should think about reinvesting some of your early profits as soon as possible. It is strongly recommended that you avoid giving in to the temptation of cashing in your gains. The goal is to increase the amount of investing cash you have available so that it can provide even higher returns.

The only disadvantage of HFT is the need to pay transaction fees. Make sure that you have a complete understanding of the fee that your broker assesses for each every trade. It's possible that your profits are being eaten up by exorbitant transaction fees. Buying in bulk is recommended in order to reduce the likelihood of being subjected to large transaction costs. For instance, your broker might provide 10 transactions for the price of $2.99 each. This kind of package gives you the ability to calculate your costs, which in turn gives you the ability to see your returns.

How to Assess Whether or Not Day Trading is Right for You

It should come as no surprise that day trading is not suitable for everyone. Day trading demands a dedication to understanding how to use the trading platform effectively in order to be profitable. By being familiar with the platform, you will be able to effectively configure all of your offers. After that, you are free to step back and allow the platform do its work.

If your goal is to become an investor who does not actively manage their portfolio, day trading is probably not the best choice for you. If you are a passive investor, you probably have no interest in actively participating in the trading process. Day trading, on the other hand, can help you become a passive investor because it just requires you to set up your trades at the beginning of each trading day. This reduces the amount of work you have to do. Your open positions will be finished off by the system before the conclusion of the trading day. In the meantime, you might use your time to plan out your next move and investigate it.

Where to put your money in mutual funds:

Fidelity Real Estate Investment Portfolio $FRESX Fidelity Select Technology Portfolio $FSPTX Vanguard U.S. Growth Fund Investor Shares $VWUSX Fidelity Real Estate Investment Portfolio $FRESX

Mutual funds, in contrast to index funds, are subject to higher costs.

0.38% per year in loss for $VWUSX

0.73% on an annual basis for $FRESX.

0.69% per year deducted from $FSPTX

The costs are not particularly expensive, and given that $FRESX delivers a yearly dividend of 1.83%, that yield alone is sufficient to cover the fees for all three funds.

Mutual funds are an excellent method of diversification since they allow you to diversify within a specific market.

You can automate this process by making recurrent investments, just like you would with index funds. However, you should be aware that mutual funds have a higher level of risk than index funds do because they are managed by other people, and portfolio changes and particular industry news can have a significant impact on the stocks in the fund. You should only allocate a tiny portion of your total investment budget to purchase mutual funds.

Funds of Hedge: A hedge fund is a pooled investment fund that trades in relatively liquid assets and can make considerable use of more complex trading, portfolio design, and risk management techniques in an effort to improve performance. These tactics include short selling, leverage, and derivatives. Hedge funds invest in a variety of assets. In a nutshell, hedge funds invest your money for you, but they do so using strategies that are more complicated and risky. This strategy is not suitable for everyone, and the only people who can use it are those with a significant amount of wealth.

The following are the requirements to invest in hedge funds:

Applicants must either have a net worth of at least $1 million (not counting their principal property) or an annual income of at least $200,000 (or $300,000 if they include the income of their spouse). As a direct consequence of this, hedge funds often have large minimum investments, which range anywhere from $100,000 to $1 million.

Hedge funds are not something I would advocate, but they are followed by some of the most knowledgeable analysts in the business. If this is something that interests you, then you should conduct additional research on the topic.

Fees for Hedge Funds:

2% of the total value of the fund's assets

16.4% performance fee An investment manager receives money for creating positive returns on an investor's capital.

The Finest Hedge Funds Available for Investment

66% average annual returns since 1988 for the Medallion fund managed by Renaissance Technologies; 39% of those returns are after expenses.

The largest hedge fund in the world, Bridgewater Associates, has been able to generate 11.5% annual returns for its investors while managing around $150 billion in capital over a period of 28 years.

Jana Partners has generated an average annual return of 17.5% from the beginning of its existence up through the end of 2019, which is the most recent year for which there is reporting on the fund's performance.

Tiger Global Management - Tiger Global Management has been recognized as one of the most successful hedge funds in the world for a number of years. From an initial investment of $8 million in the year 1980, the company eventually amassed $22 billion in assets by the late 1990s. Returning 22.4% yearly between the years 2016 and the middle of 2019.

Robo-Advisors: A Robo-advisor is a digital financial advisor that offers financial advice or manages investments with moderate to minimal human participation. Robo-advisors have become increasingly popular in recent years. Robo-advisors are computer programs that are programmed to provide investment guidance to clients in a digital format depending on the information provided by the client. It's as easy as that; algorithms will build you a portfolio that's tailored to your preferences, and the fees are surprisingly low, ranging from 0% to 0.75 %. The fact that your portfolio is maintained entirely online and trades are carried out on their own accord makes this the least research-intensive manner of investing possible.

Status report on Jenna

Today, she is pursuing a partners degree in word-related treatment at a school where she is currently enrolled. A decentralized creative and public speaker, she has the attention of people all around the world. Very helpful for a child who, at the age of sixteen, was reading and writing at a level equivalent to the second grade. (She was diagnosed with high-risk leukemia when she was a very young child and endured harsh chemotherapy to fight the disease. She also suffered epileptic seizures between the ages of eight and twelve.) She was deprived of the first thirteen years that make up the life of a "typical" youngster. brave, goal-oriented, unyielding, and persistent; a competitor. My sweetheart.

What I have come to understand is... A strong network or set of affiliations is the most important factor to consider while trying to plan for a secure financial future. In the same vein, it is the capital resource that is the least exploited. Who you know is of the utmost importance.

The most challenging aspect of turning land into a profitable investment is developing connections, which is also the primary reason why so many first-time investors are unsuccessful. They make an effort to complete everything on their own. To establish these fundamental linkages calls for an initial financial outlay in addition to hard work. The importance of this component is overlooked by many.

Why do you act in the manner that you do?

" David," a variety of dental specialists have asked me, "for what reason aren't you resigned?" They are asking why you continue to work so hard given that you apparently done so well with land and dentistry. Investigate properly. In point of fact, there is nothing—absolutely nothing—that is expected of me at all. My current line of work is the primary means by which I am able to make a positive contribution with the time I have available. The thing that requires my consideration is an honest enthusiasm for assisting my partners in breaking the chains of being captives to their practices, their financial sentiments of anxiety, and assisting them with making opportunity in both their day-to-day lives and the lives of their families. I adore the fact that this provides me with a stage and invites some of the most outstanding and accomplished people in the fields of business, advertising, real estate, and finance to Dallas on a quarterly basis throughout the year. This particular set of folks is my most effective kind of defense. In light of the unpredictability and questions that surround our economy and our sector, putting together a Board of Advisors gives us the opportunity to step apart from the fallout and examine the opportunities that are presented by mayhem. Due to the fact that I am involved in all of the land opportunities within our organization, I am able to make agreements and assist our members in utilizing the various forms of investment cash in the most secure, typically efficient, and effective manner that is possible.

Being in a position to quit and really stepping down from my position are two whole different things for me. It's highly unlikely that I'll ever resign in the traditional sense. Maintaining my position as a crucial and significant player until both my body and my mind give out, because it sounds amazing! My social circle and connections put me in a position where I can accomplish precisely that. What a blessing!

The Brokers

When talking about markets, you should pay particular attention to brokers because they are the ones that allow you access to those marketplaces. The majority of beginning investors have a healthy amount of skepticism against brokers, but for the wrong reasons. In most cases, people have the misconception that a broker is plotting against them or attempting to undermine them in some way. This is not true because the consequences for breaking FINRA's guidelines are severe, and no broker is going to risk losing their reputation by engaging in behavior like this.

This does not, however, imply that your broker is your closest confidante. They are separate companies whose sole purpose is to generate profits, and the primary manner in which they achieve this is by encouraging you to engage in financial dealings with them. Your broker will be in a stronger financial position the more you trade. Because of this, many brokers urge their customers to make as many trades as they possibly can, providing them with trading ideas through newsletters and other means.

App-based brokers take it one step further by making the experience more like a game, and in general, they lose any feeling of fiduciary duty they may have had toward their customers. They portray the market as a casino, suggesting that everyone should gamble all the time in order to maximize their chances of making money. This is done in the name of expanding investing opportunities "to the small guy." They fail to see the need of educating their customers, thus as a result, their customers are led to believe that investing and gambling are the same thing.

It is in your best interest to steer clear of shady brokers such as these and focus your business on organizations that have been in business for more than ten years. Because membership in FINRA is a prerequisite for being a broker, you should look for one that has this certification. You should not rely on your broker for financial advice because they are not qualified to offer advice and know about the market as much as your dog does. Instead, look elsewhere for financial guidance.

If you are looking for guidance, the best thing you can do is educate yourself or talk to a financial consultant who is registered with the government. In addition to traditional brokerage services; larger brokerage firms like Charles Schwab also provide financial advising services. The catch is that the minimum investment required with such brokers is rather expensive, and it is typically over $25,000 in most cases.

There are a great number of online discount brokers, and the majority of them have account minimums that are lower than $100. Therefore, going with them is a smart decision in this regard. Even while you can't expect these brokers to stop sending you emails that encourage you to trade, you can go in the right way by deciding not to download their apps on your device.

You don't need an app on your phone to trade properly, and you don't need to trade all the time or "stay up to date" with the markets. All you need to do is trade when it makes sense for you. The only SEC filings that investors need to pay attention to are those that are directly related to their investments; yet, you can't read these documents on your phone even if you tried. If you stick to the desktop version, you won't be tempted to trade all the time because you won't have access to the mobile app.

Access to options trading is provided to novice investors by a variety of brokers nowadays. Even though you have the ability to trade options, you should avoid doing so. These methods are extremely different from the normal YOLO trades that you will see on social media, and I will describe some of them later in this book. However, there are a few strategies that you can deploy utilizing options, and I will discuss some of them later in this book.

All that is required to make profitable investments is a cash account. This is a fundamental investment account that you will automatically be provided with by your broker. The required minimum balance for these accounts is typically relatively low and does not constitute a significant obstacle. There are even brokers who don't require any sort of minimum balance.

Before you commit to opening an account with a broker, you should be sure to read the reviews the broker has received and ask them questions. Concerning yourself just with a broker's customer service is truly all that is required of you. Before you make any transactions, you should first spend some time getting acquainted with their program. It is important to keep in mind that there is no rush to place trades, and that you do not need to keep a high level of activity in order to be successful.

If you feel pressure from your broker to always be trading, you have the option to switch to another broker who will not make you feel the same way. It will not be necessary for you to sell those shares and then purchase them again because your previous broker will instantly transfer them to your new broker.

Our discussion of the markets and the dynamics of investment has come to an end with this point. Because the information contained in this on investment operations is very important for you to comprehend, you should make sure to read the material contained here more than once.

How Exactly Does One Go About Making Money Off Of Stocks?

In the long run, it could be beneficial for you to have an understanding of how tick works. There are two different applications for them that can be used to generate income for you. When the value of the stock you have purchased increases, you will be able to sell it for a profit and pocket the cash. When the value of the stock first starts to go up, it is the optimal time to sell it. Because the value of the stocks fluctuates over time, it is in your best interest to take any profits you have made by selling the stocks before they reach their full potential.

The other method by which you might profit from 'tock' is by receiving dividends. The term "dividend" refers to the payments that a corporation makes to its shareholders on a regular basis. The dividends often serve as a reflection of the company's earnings and are typically computed based on the company's aid earnings. The dividend may or may not be paid out, depending on the kind of stock that was purchased by the investor. One useful piece of advice I can offer is to reinvest dividends by purchasing additional shares of stock so as to boost one's overall return. You have the option of enrolling in a plan that focuses on dividend investments.

Choosing When It Is Most Appropriate To Do Business With

Timing is of the utmost importance when it comes to the market. If you want to profit from your stocks, you will need to decide in advance whether you will buy them or sell them in order to maximize your earnings. There are a variety of "strategies" that you can employ to decide when the best time is to trade.

Strategy of Buying Low and Selling High

There is a strategy known as "buy low and sell high," and investors typically use this one. However, it is extremely difficult to accurately predict when the stock will be at a low price and when it will be at a high price. You can decide to use the principle of supply and demand to determine when the best time is to trade, despite the fact that there is no method that has been proved to accurately estimate the optimal trading time. According to the theory of supply and demand, when there is a high demand for a particular stock, there is also a high supply of that stock, and vice versa.

Techniques For Timing The Market And The Buy-And-Hold Strategy

The other method is called market timing, and it involves making forecasts about how stocks will trade in the future by using either fundamental or technical analysis. This method is fraught with peril because there are a number of unforeseeable factors that could have an impact on the value of the stock. The buy-and-hold strategy is yet another method that the majority of investors employ. This technique focuses on purchasing stocks at a time that is not always when their prices are at their lowest and then keeping those equities until the time is right to sell them. People who use this tactic to gain money almost always end up with large returns, in contrast to those who try to time the market.

Investors have been subjected to a constant barrage of information regarding stock investing from various financial media outlets. This information has been plentiful. This deluge of information is being spread over a variety of different media sources. Although some of these industry resources provide useful information, the report may not be of much use in arriving at an informed decision. Studies have demonstrated that the Value line, with its extremely sophisticated analysis, is unable to come close to competing with the Market index. According to the findings of the research, in order to beat the Market index, one needs to perform "superior" analysis and execute at the appropriate times. The term used for this one-of-a-kind "kill" is "Alpha," and here is an example of Alpha looking for a fight. Gurus include individuals such as Warren

Buffett, George Soros, Peter Lynch, and others.

It is necessary to first establish the various categories of stock investing before entering into a more pragmatic framework of stocks. Common stocks and preferred stocks are the two primary types of equities available to investors. The primary distinction between the two can be summed up as follows: first, preferred stocks have an advantage over common stocks in terms of the shareholders' ability to file a claim against the company in the event of a breach of contract on the part of the business. Second, preferred stocks are bought in order to receive dividends (a form of income), but they offer a lower possibility for capital appreciation. Common stocks, on the other hand, can be used for both dividends and capital appreciation, with the emphasis being placed on the latter. Third, preferred stocks can behave similarly to bonds in some circumstances; for example, if interest rates were to rise, the price of preferred stocks would typically fall. The variation in interest rates has some degree of a correlation with the overall stock market. This is due to the fact that when interest rates rise, the stock market suffers the consequences. The effects that changes in interest rates will have on individual common stocks will be determined by a number of factors, the most important of which is the capital (or debt) structure of the company.

The following are some examples of other categories of common "tock": The first stocks of a reputable blue chip company Companies listed on the Dow Jones that have a proven track record of providing dividends to shareholders. Second, value stocks are undervalued gems that have a good chance of growing in value over the long term. Third, growth stocks are growth-oriented stocks that are valued higher due to investors' expectations of increased appreciation in the future. As their name suggests, growth stocks are priced higher. The fourth type of tick is cyclical ticks, which are sensitive to variations in the business cycles. And finally, "tock," which means "be calm throughout market "wing," "such a" Utilities.

The Concept Of Money As Raw Data

If you are knowledgeable about the web, you probably understand what I mean when I say "cash as a substance type." I am referring to monetary value that is transmitted in its entirety in the form of information and can be transferred by any mode of communication that is able to convey information.

Despite the fact that doing so directly to the Bitcoin organization is a beneficial manner of doing so, a bitcoin exchange should not be sent directly to the Bitcoin organization. You might encrypt it using the emoticons available on Skype. You might write a review of it and then include it in a campaign on Craigslist. You could share it on Facebook as a behind-the-scenes look at an image showing some kittens interacting with some yarn.

Money has transitioned into the form of raw data, which is being streamed on an organization that is simultaneously unable to be censored, available to anybody, objective, and global in scope. This brand-new innovation does not feature any waiting in line, very similar to how the internet does not feature any waiting in line.

Due to the fact that Bitcoin is neither a physical good nor a company, anyone can have access to it. You are not need to sign up in order to obtain a record. You are downloading a consumer into your system. You can participate in a global economy by downloading just one program; this global economy is open to people of every race, religion, ideology, nationality, age, and sexual orientation wherever in the world.

This concept has not yet fully taken hold in the minds of a significant number of individuals. It's possible that children born today won't have a clue about a world in which there are banks, a world in which paper money is used as currency, or anything else that the younger people working in our sector today know about what the world was like before the internet. How many of you have memories of visiting libraries and going at reference cards? Okay, so you're well into your forties at this point. I am as well. You fool!

The children who are being created right now may never use a motor car or live in a world without the internet. They also won't ever know what it's like to live in a society in which banks control the money supply and only national governments are able to distribute it. Because money is a sort of content that can be conveyed by anyone, anytime, it will inevitably become an essential convention on the web.

However, it is clearly not the case. We need to make it a more enjoyable experience.

1.2.2 The Role of Money as Its Own Independent System

Up until this point, every form of monetary exchange required a person to stand behind it. Prior to that, funds must be claimed and supervised by individuals, or persons collectively framing an affiliation, which is referred to as the organization. This is a legal fiction. However, Bitcoin is merely an agreement. It is designed for self-employed professionals to use in order to claim and manage their own funds. There is no need for certain individuals. Imagine a corporation that does not have any CEOs, investors, or representatives and that is entirely dependent on pre-programmed AI or possibly simply a couple of basic heuristic standards. This corporation operates independently of any human activity and is in charge of budgets that are in the billions of millions.

And at this time, the audience is divided into two distinct groups. There are some individuals who are considering, "Oh, no!" That makes a horrible sound. What if it turns out to be a virus? What if it's clever ransomware that can self-proliferate and buys systems from Amazon Web Service so that it can expand when it's successful? What if it begins to improve itself by recruiting new programmers and putting themselves through A/B testing?

Indeed, every one of those things is going to come to pass. But what if it's an intelligent charity that can identify the onset of a natural disaster and then immediately and automatically reroute significant sums of money to the people who need them the most without any assistance from a human? And in contrast to the majority of organizations operating in the modern world, each and every dollar contributed would be distributed to individuals in need.

The world is going to go through a transition.

Vehicles that drive themselves? What about autos that don't require a claim? Despite the fact that they are not claimed by an enterprise, certain automobiles have been identified as belonging to a particular business. Cars that pay for their electricity or gas costs, as well as their maintenance and rental fees, by delivering rides to customers who pay them in digital currencies like as bitcoin or ethereum.

Imagine the code as insightful pieces that spread over the web as content and, as more people read them, extend their reach farther. This is what we mean by programming. As a consequence of this, they are now in a position to acquire additional facilitating services, which will allow them to further expand their customer base.

Advantages Of Purchasing Covered Call Options

The first advantage of covered call options is that the trader selling the option receives a premium payment, which can be kept as income regardless of whether or not the trader exercises their option to buy or sell the underlying asset. Serious investors in markets that are reasonably neutral or positive have the opportunity to establish this as a regular cash flow for their portfolios. The investor has the ability to devise a plan that will involve the consistent sale of covered calls. This has the ability to establish a reoccurring income stream on a monthly or quarterly basis.

The second advantage of covered calls is that investors can use them to help target a higher selling price for a specific stock than the price at which the stock is currently trading. The last advantage of covered calls is that they reduce the seller's exposure to risk because the underlying asset acts as a buffer in the transaction.

The Dangers Involved When Investing in Covered Call Options

If the stock price falls below the break-even point, the seller of the covered call is subject to financial loss. This is the primary and most significant risk involved with covered calls. Everyone who invests in the stock market is subject to this risk.

The inability to accurately forecast a significant increase in the stock's price constitutes the second potential loss. However, if the holder of the options for that stock decides to exercise his or her right, then the seller is obligated to transfer the stock to the person who exercised their option. Stocks have an endless potential for profit. Because of this, the seller will need to hand over a significant asset throughout the deal, which may result in the loss of a fantastic opportunity.

The Step-by-Step Guide to Creating a Covered Call Option

The purchase of the underlying stock is the initial stage in the process of constructing a covered call. This is accomplished by acquiring it in increments of one hundred shares at a time. You will be able to sell an option for every 100 shares of stock if you proceed in this manner. When you acquire stocks in this manner, you do not need to option any of them, which is one of the many benefits of doing so. Take, for instance, the scenario in which you purchased 1000 shares of stock. You have the ability to sell 5 contracts, which will allow you to leverage 500 shares and receive 5 premium payments. Even if the people who now possess the options on those 5 contracts decide to exercise their right, you will still keep control of the 500 shares of stock.

The final thing that needs to be done is to wait for the covered call to either be exercised or to run out of time. In the event that the covered calls are not put into action, you will be allowed to keep the premium. Although there is always the opportunity to buy back the option before the expiration date approaches, sellers almost never take use of this provision. It is important to keep in mind that once you have an option on a stock, you must be willing to sell it.

Obtaining Financial Support and Conceiving Original Concepts

Putting down twenty percent of the purchase price and borrowing the remaining eighty percent was the conventional approach to financing real estate purchases for many years. Of course, you had the option to put down more money, but the standard minimum down payment is twenty percent. Thankfully, this used to be the norm, but times have changed.

These days, investors in real estate have access to a wide array of financing options to choose from. When it comes to funding your purchase, a second mortgage is a frequent method. The buyer makes a down payment equal to five percent of the purchase price and borrows the remaining fifteen percent through a separate loan at a rate of interest that is typically higher.

Even while it's to your favor to pay a lower price for a house, the fact that you'll have to pay a higher interest rate isn't the only negative aspect. When a buyer does not meet the minimum down payment requirement of 20%, they are typically required to pay for expensive private mortgage insurance, abbreviated as PMI.

The private mortgage insurance (PMI) policy can be cancelled whenever the loan-to-value (LTV) ratio reaches 80%.

It is possible to achieve this goal by reducing the amount owed on the second mortgage and by raising the property's value. This occurs quite infrequently due to the fact that the buyer typically re-finances or sells the house before the PMI may be cancelled.

Innovative investors have access to a variety of additional funding possibilities. Homebuilders participating in planned developments are typically willing to provide financing to first-time buyers of their properties.

The financing strategy known as "sub2," which is an abbreviation for "subject-to," is yet another risky and challenging option for purchasing real estate. You will receive the deed to the property from the seller, but the loan will continue to be held by the lending institution. The buyer will solely be responsible for making payments on the loan. This kind of transaction can be carried out in a number of different ways. Because of the complexity and potential for loss associated with this method of funding an investment, it is not recommended for those with less experience.

Joining a limited partnership as a means of funding your real estate venture is another option worth considering. There are a number of applications for this strategy that can be taken. In certain cases, all members of the partnership are expected to make a financial contribution, often equal to half of the total cost. However, the profit is sometimes distributed in a manner that is not directly proportional to the initial amount that was placed. Alternately, it is possible for one half of the partnership to supply the cash, while the other half is responsible for providing the necessary services, such as repairing the house. There are a number of applications for this strategy that can be taken.

Veterans and low-income investors who have served their country in the armed forces may be eligible for financing from the government. In most cases, these programs are restricted to just being available for primary residences.

Have you ever given any thought to paying for the purchase of a home with a credit card? This is still another way to finance the purchase of real estate; nevertheless, in most cases, it is not a good idea to go this route. The majority of interest rates on credit cards are plainly a lot greater than the interest rates on loans. A further drawback is that lenders determine your creditworthiness based on your continuous debt; hence, if you use credit card cash advances to satisfy the needed 5-20% down payment, you will most likely be denied a loan. This is because lenders evaluate your creditworthiness based on your ongoing debt. This is likewise the case with money that is borrowed from friends or relatives, unless you can provide evidence that the money was actually given to you as a gift.

Your Objectives And The Amount Of Money That Will Be Necessary

When you first start investing, one of the most crucial things you should do is make sure that the money you invest is not going to be utilized for any other finances. It is quite unfortunate, but one of the reasons why Americans save so little in comparison to people in other parts of the world is because they typically keep their savings and their funds for unexpected expenses in the same bank account. To avoid finding yourself in this predicament, you should ensure that the money you are putting into investments is money that you can put away and forget about for a period of 10 years. This is something that will ultimately depend on your business plan and how you intend to put the money that you are investing to use. Due to the time lock that is connected with each investment option, a government bond or a 529 plan are both excellent choices for first-time investors. It is in your best interest to wait until your child is ready for college before withdrawing money from a 529 plan because the plan assesses a fee for withdrawals that aren't linked to education, and a government bond simply won't pay out until the date on the bond has passed. Your business plan should include an estimate of the amount of profit you anticipate making from each individual investment. This kind of strategy provides you with a timeframe as well as a list of important targets to achieve at various stages along the way. It is essential to include this in your plan in order to keep track of how far you have come toward achieving your objectives, whether those objectives involve saving money for retirement, college, or a home.

Determine the Number of Hours Per Week That You Are Able to Invest.

Understanding how much time you can devote to this task is just as vital as being aware of your goals and locating the appropriate investment options, all of which are important in their own right. In recent years, currency trading on the FOREX market has gained a lot of popularity. The foreign currency exchange markets, also known as FOREX, are becoming increasingly popular due to the fact that investors can participate in day-to-day trading. There are a lot of FOREX traders that choose to hold long positions, but the majority of trades are completed in a relatively short period of time, and traders are able to keep track of how much money they make each day. This type of investment project is best appreciated by those who have a lot of spare time to research, observe trends, and pull out at the appropriate time. While this may sound thrilling, it is best enjoyed by those who have a lot of free time. Those individuals who prefer to make changes to their assets on a weekly or monthly basis but simply are unable to commit the required number of hours per day for FOREX trading might consider making their investments in the stock market instead.

Those individuals who do not have the time to engage in individual stocks or the FOREX market might take advantage of investment opportunities such as 529 programs, government bonds, and index funds instead. Regardless of whether you want to participate in currency trading on the foreign exchange market or not, I strongly advise you to make an additional investment in a program with a longer duration. You will not earn an extremely high interest rate with a government bond; however, it is the safest investment you can make, and in terms of sticking to your financial plan, you will know the exact day that you will receive your money and the precise amount that you will receive when you invest in a government bond. You should begin your investment strategy with U.S. treasury bonds and possibly an index fund if you are absolutely confused how to proceed with investments. Although mutual funds are a popular choice for investing, the interest that can be generated from them is not particularly compelling. Mutual funds are nothing more than a collection of stocks, and their decisions are made by individual investors. Because of this, mutual funds are considered to be a high-risk investing option, and they are not recommended for investors who do not wish to spend a significant amount of time monitoring their investments.

www.ingramcontent.com/pod-product-compliance
Lightning Source LLC
Chambersburg PA
CBHW011843200326
41597CB00026B/4680